Is it Religion or Relationship?

Julie Hazel

Ark House Press
arkhousepress.com

AMG Pubs. (1996). The Hebrew-Greek Key Word Study Bible, New International Version.

Cataloguing in Publication Data:
Title: Is It Religion Or Relationship?
ISBN: 978-1-7642813-8-6 (pbk)
Subjects: [REL012120]   RELIGION / Christian Living / Spiritual Growth; [REL030000]   RELIGION / Christian Ministry / Evangelism; [REL023000] RELIGION / Christian Ministry / Discipleship.

Design by initiateagency.com

Dear Reader,

Do you have a relationship with the Triune God? Have a think about these things while you read the book.

The world is in such a muddle, the end, is not far away and therefore our relationship with Triune God has to be on solid ground, the ground of the Kingdom of God.

Jesus didn't know when the end of this present age would be. Only God the Father knows this. Jesus tells us, *'No-one knows about that day or hour, not even the angels in heaven nor the Son but only the Father.'* Matthew 24:36

Iain M Duguid, says, "Have you received the transplant of righteousness that comes through Jesus Christ?"

God Bless in and through Jesus Christ.

Julie

contents

one

God the Father made each of us human beings to have a free will and so, when we make decisions, there will be consequences in the now and into the future. There are also the consequences for the decisions we have made in the past. The decisions we make in the soul, which is our mind, will and emotions, have consequences that effect our soul and the physical life as well those who are close to us. These consequences can have a positive or negative result of good and bad.

Decisions we make in our human spirits can have monumental results. You see, the human spirit was made to be in contact with God who is loving and good. But we are fallen creatures living in a fallen world and are easily lead, especially by evil, even when we think we are doing good.

When I asked Jesus to my Saviour I just assumed that I had just turnover a new leaf even though it was God the Holy Spirit who had made contact with me and he was going to continue with me through the good the bad and ugly of my life and into eternity. The benefits of the indwelling Holy Spirit will of course will worked out in each one God's children a little differently, but always to the glory of God.

In my work life and early part of my Christian life. I considered myself working for the glory of God, studying and working educating myself as well as doing some Christian duties. The Spirit showed me that my so-called obedience was only cultural thought. God the Father was about to show me many things I didn't know or understand before.

Most people realise the world around them is becoming more and more dangerous but we have no idea without God's Holy Spirit guiding us spiritually, soulically and physically what to really think and do about it. Human beings are becoming more and more self-centered unloving and uncaring and are easily lead into evil, but we must realise that we are be responsible for our own sin, not someone else.

There is a spiritually evil person and this person is Satan, he is also known as the devil. Some consider Satan to be as powerful as God, this is one thing that I learnt was not true. However, over the years, I have met many people who believe Satan is as powerful God, or even more powerful.

The Jungle Doctor, answering the question of a small boy who asks, "Are the curses of the devil stronger than the powers of God? The doctor says, 'I'll answer that, if you can answer me this, 'is the strength of the hyena to be compared with that of the lion? 'Surely the lion.' says the boy."

However, this does not take away from the fact Satan is evil.

You may ask, who is he? He was an angel created by God, however he wanted to be God instead of worshipping and obeying God. There are a couple of Old Testament passages in two prophesies that also alludes to Satan as well. The first is from Isaiah, *'I will ascend above the tops of the clouds, I will make myself like the Most High.'* And second, is from Ezekiel, *'Your heart became proud on the account of your beauty and you corrupted your wisdom because of your splendor. So, I threw you down to the earth, I made a spectacle of you before kings.'* Satan has corrupted the whole world including you and me.

These days, many people do not believe that there is the One True God or that the Bible is the true written word of God. And that everything written in it is the truth. When it comes thinking and talking about God there is a lot that is outside the limits of our minds and understanding and we have to take God at his word, this is where faith in God who is the Truth comes to the rescue.

An illustration concerning faith in God is seen in Acts with Barnabas and the Christians at Antioch. The persecution of the Christians had started with the stoning of Stephen and they were scattered.

Different Christians started to tell, evangelising (*euangelizo*) the gospel in different places. The Spirit God took some to Antioch where there became a multicultural church of brothers and sisters. This is where the church in Jerusalem sent Barnabas. *'When he arrived and saw the evidence of the grace of God, he was glad and encouraged them to all to remain true to the Lord with all their hearts. He was a good man full of the Holy Spirit and faith, and a great number of people were brought to the Lord.'* Not only had they gone on to accepted Jesus as Saviour but also as Lord of their lives through into eternity.

The reality is that we humans have no concept or understanding of the true God without the power and guidance of the Holy Spirit of God. In fact, most of the time we do not want to know or care about God in any shape or form, we are too wrapped up in ourselves and our own so- called realities. Or we want to have God our way on our terms, in other words, religion.

In today's world many people are saying they asked Jesus to be their Saviour. Bingo! A reality check! Has God really made contact with them and guided them through the Holy Spirit to accept they are in desperate need of Jesus Christ as Saviour and Lord of their lives? "It isn't enough to know about God", we need to know God, Father, Son and Holy Spirit who is the Triune God as our God.

We need to confess that we are a sinner and need to be saved. Believe that Jesus Christ is the Son of God and acknowledge Jesus Christ, died for their sin and rose again from the dead to give them eternal life to all who ask and believe Jesus Christ as Saviour and Lord of our lives. We need to be allowing God to be the center of our lives. The center of reality is Father, Son and Holy Spirit. In that case, reality is much bigger and more powerful than anything we have ever considered or will ever considered without God.

Lewis says, "If Christianity was something we were making up, of course we could make it easier. But it is not. We cannot compete in simplicity with people who are inventing religions. How could we? We are dealing with facts, of course anyone can be simple if he does not have any facts to bother with."

So then, what are facts? A fact is a thing asserted to be true as a basis for reasoning. In this day and age we need to ask ourselves, is our reasoning only based subjectively on what we think, or is it really objective, in other words is it based on what God has said?

We must base our reasoning only on, a relationship with God. *'The Lord our God, the Lord is one. Love the Lord with all your heart and with all your soul and with all your strength.'*

The English word 'God' is for Father, Son and Holy Spirit. And in the Hebrew, it is *Yahweh*. The word one, means unity, meaning a relationship,

He is one God, however he is three Persons. We see this in the command Jesus gives to the disciples, *'Go and make disciples of all nations baptising them in the name of the Father, and of the Son and the Holy Spirit.'* Trinity means, three-ness and speaks of God as Father, Son and Holy Spirit. Using the unity of the Godhead in the baptising the children of God confirming to them, that they are truly in a loving relationship with the Almighty God.

We need to take a step out of the religious way of thinking about Christianity and bring our thoughts into a relationship with the Triune God. The relationship of the

Father, Son and Holy Spirit has always been a relationship of Agape love, from all eternity and will continue through all eternity. Bringing all who belong to him into the indwelling of Father, Son and Holy Spirit in our human spirits. Continuing to draw down into our souls and physical body.

Johnson says, "The living God is not a solitary God. The living God is not a isolated God. From all eternity the living God has lived in relationship, indeed, has lived as relationship. At the center of the universe is relationship. From all eternity the living God has been community, family. From all eternity the living God has been infinitely pleased as Father, Son and Holy Spirit".

One God, but three Persons who are inter connected in love and truth. There is a Triune relationship, Father, Son and Holy Spirit who are eternal, who is, who always has been and who will always be, with the essence of holiness and substance of love and truth at the center his being.

The Trinity is not a matter for debate or even attempted explanation, but for a reverent acceptance. A reverence acceptance accepts God the Father who planned the creation of the universe and because of His great love for humanity planned the salvation of us humans before the creation of the world by sending the Son to take the sin of humanity in His being and dying on the cross to pay the price for our sin. Rising from the dead to bring salvation to all who believe in his name. With the third Person of the Trinity, the Holy Spirit. Who was at the beginning of creation and who was with Jesus in his earthly ministry and he was with the disciples after Pentecost and he is with all who believe on the name of Jesus today.

Out of this relationship of love of Father, Son and Holy Spirit, humanity was created and redeemed however most of humanity past, present and future will never accept being redeemed by another, let alone Jesus Christ for we are sinners, thinking we bosses of our lives but living in a fallen world with a sinful worldly system under the influence Satan.

Why did humanity needed to be redeemed? First, redeem means to be brought back. Why? The answer is very simple, our ancestor Adam chose to disobey God to please himself. Eve was deceived by Satan however Adam disobeyed God. And this disobedience has continued to be passed down to each generation to us today.

God had commanded Adam not to eat the fruit from the tree of the knowledge of good and evil, this was before God created Eve. *'The Lord God took the man and put him in the Garden of Eden to work it and to take care of it. And the Lord God commanded the man, you are free to eat from any tree in the garden but you must not eat from the tree of the knowledge of good and evil, for when you eat from it you will certainly die.'* And each generation continues to die.

The consequences of Adam's sin continues today *'Whoever believes in him* (Jesus Christ), *is not condemned but whoever does not believe stands condemned already because he has not believed in the name of God's one and only Son.'*

It is like as if we, the Christian, have been given the key to the bank vault, however we must realise the treasure is worth more than the vault full of gold bars 'There is one God and one Mediator between God man (humanity) the man Jesus Christ.' Jesus Christ, fully God and fully human sacrificed himself. He, as the intercessory, became the surety, the security for the debt God had on humanity, even before the beginning of the world.

Now the Holy Spirit the Spirit of Christ, 'who is the deposit guaranteeing our inheritance until the redemption of those who are God's possession, to his praise and glory.'

Humanity, even those of us who seek Jesus would prefer to do it on our own terms than on God the Father's terms. Nevertheless, Jesus Christ is the only guarantor of the new covenant in his blood. He is the King of the universe, not Satan or self.

We must realise it was for our benefit that God the Father's relationship with the Son was opened the way for the Son to have died and to rise again for all of those who would believe through the guidance of God's the Holy Spirit in the name of Jesus Christ. The Holy Spirit brings the individual under the power of the gospel of Jesus Christ for salvation. 'You were also included in Christ when you heard the word of truth, the gospel of your salvation'.

The so called modern Christian religions where preachers say that all we need to do is ask Jesus to our Saviour and we will be saved, in a way that is partly true however, it leaves out the reality that God is to be Lord of our lives now! We are not to go on planning and living the rest of our lives as we choose and then expect to be going with Jesus at the end of our lives. Jesus, tells us, *'Not everyone who says to me, Lord, Lord will enter the Kingdom heaven, only he who does the will of my Father who is in heaven. Many will say to me on that day Lord, Lord did we not prophesy in your name and in your name drive out demons and perform many miracles. Then I will tell them plainly, I never knew you.'*

He will not know those who call themselves Christians and do his so-called works but leave him out of the picture.

Here we have encouragement, *'but if we walk in the light, as he is in the light, we have fellowship with one another and the blood of Jesus his Son purifies us from all sin. If we claim to be without sin, we deceive ourselves and the truth is not in us. If we confess our sins, he is faithful and just and will forgive us our sins and purify us from all unrighteousness. If we claim we have not sinned we make him out to be a liar and his word has no place in our lives.'*

If the Word of God has no place in our lives, then we cannot have a relationship with God now and therefore we will have no place with him in eternity

PRENOTE

Matthew 28:39

Duguid I

NOTES

White Paul, Jungle Doctor on the Hop, Christian Focus Publications, Australia 2006, p 141.

Isaiah 14: 14

Ezekiel 28:17

Acts 11:23-24

White Paul, Jungle Doctor's Crooked Dealings, Christian Focus Publications, Australia, 2008, p 103.

Lewis Clive S., Mere Christianity, 1952, pp141. Collins Fount Paperback

The Australian Modern Oxford Dictionary, Oxford university Press, 1998

Deuteronomy 6:4

Matthew 28:19

Jeffery Peter, Bitesize Theology, p61, EP Books, England

Johnson Darrell quoting Tertullian, pp61, 1947, Experiencing The Trinity, Regent Publishing

Peter Jeffery, Bitesize Theology, pp34, Bitesize Theology, EP
    Books England

Genesis 2:15-17

John 3:18

1Timothy 2:5.

Ephesians 1:14

Ephesians 1:13

Matthew 7:22-23

1John 1:7-10

TWO

About thirty years ago I heard the parable of The Sower preached in such a way I learnt many true things that was missing from my understanding of a relationship with God.

When I was young woman, I started going to a modern church and in the course of time I asked Jesus to be my Savior. However, I had heard nothing of asking Jesus Christ to be Lord of my life as well. I would say, that there are many today who assume that because they have ask Jesus to be Saviour and that everything is ok, and can get on running the rest of their lives, as long their moral lives are reasonably Christian like.

When Jesus was on earth he told many parables, with the truth and reality within stories. The parable of the

Sower in Luke, in which he tells the parable to the crowd and then afterwards he tells his disciples the great truths hidden in verses further along, as the disciples wanted to know these great truths, this is still the same today if we want to know, God will guide us in the way of truth.

At the time of this parable, the farmer would sprinkle the seeds of his crop over the ground and it would go everywhere, and then he ploughed it in to the good soil where he wanted the plants to grow and waited for his crop to grow. The Word of God, is the seed, through which the Holy Spirit scatters it in the hearts and souls of the hearers especially, whose hearts and souls of those he has prepared for the planting the seed of the gospel of Jesus Christ.

'Those along the path are the ones who hear and then the devil comes and takes away the wood from their hearts'. The path is a hard place for the heart to be. It can be a down trodden place, for a downtrodden heart or a place where the mean, hard and self-centered hearts are to be found. Satan opposes God's authority at every advantage place, to stop any nourishing and empowering love to the down trodden heart or God's authoritative love to a mean, hard and self-centered hearts.

The rocky ground can be many things in our day and age, from persecution and opposition through to the most wonderful proportions in the world. It becomes the testing place and time. And a time of compromise or even a change of heart. This could be because the heart wants to accepted the gospel with joy, however the mind gets in the way with the so-called common sense. But it does not consider the trouble that may come and therefore finds it difficult to cope with the realities of the Christian life and falls away from Jesus who is Life and Light of the believer.

In today's world of thorns, it is very difficult to hear the gospel of truth and respond spiritually through the empowerment of the Holy Spirit to Jesus Christ. We have those who preach their own theories of what the gospel of Jesus Christ is like. And also, when we ourselves come under the preaching of the true gospel we sometimes tend to bring our own ideas and change some truth in our minds for falsehood without realising what we are doing. Even though the soil of the heart is good enough to grow the thorns and the grains, but the grains do not mature, and the thorns being much stronger than the grains, they chock them to death. Causing the truth of the gospel of Jesus Christ to be chock out of us.

The Greek word for 'life' is *bios*, which means the manner of the business of life. We see Paul encouraging Timothy in the business of the Christian's life business. 'You then my son, be strong in the grace that is in Jesus

Christ. And the things you have heard me say in the presence of many witnesses, entrusted to reliable men (people) who will also be qualified to teach others. Join with me in suffering like a good soldier of Jesus Christ. No-one serving as a soldier gets entangled in civilian affairs, but rather tries to please his commanding officer.' Our commanding officer is the Triune God, Father, Son and Holy Spirit. In today's world the Christian's life business is not what we think, but what God knows and wills for each believer.

Jesus starts to tell the disciples the great truths hidden in the parable, *'Still, other seed fells on the good soil. It came up and yielded a crop a hundred times more than was sown. 'But, seed on the good soil stands for those with a noble and good heart, who hear the word, retain it and by persevering produce a nourishing and generous crop.'*

God's idea of a generous crop is nothing like what we think a generous is. Our thoughts are contaminated by our worldly thoughts. We need to ask the Father through his Spirit what he wants from each one of us. The right spiritual condition is to have Jesus Christ as our Savior and Lord of our lives. This is done through the guidance and power of the Holy Spirit in the name of Jesus Christ.

NOTES

Luke 8:12

2 Timothy 2:1-4

Luke 8:15

Three

Watchman Nee says in concerning salvation,
"Two aspects of salvation are presented to us,
firstly, the forgiveness of our sins, secondly,
deliverance from sin."

Concerning sin, I have two problems, I need
forgiveness of my sins I commit and I need deliverance
from the power of sin. But I belong to the first man's race,
Adam sold as a slave to sin. Every decision I make sin
deceives me and the consequences is continuing slavery
to sin. 'The heart is deceitful above all things and beyond
cure. Who can understand it?' God has redeemed those
who believe on the name of Jesus Christ, he has bought
us back from Satan. This has already been done, *with the
precious blood of Christ, a lamb without blemish or defect.'*

This is why you and I can be sinners saved by the grace of God. In the name of Jesus Christ through the power of indwelling Holy Spirit.

I am a sinner saved by God and only by the grace of God. And in the name Jesus Christ my past sin is not counted against me. *'God demonstrated his own love for us in is; while we were still sinners, Christ died for us. Since we now have been justified by his blood, how much more shall we be saved from God's wrath through him. For if when we were God's enemies, we were reconciled to him through the death of his Son how much more having been reconciled shall we be saved through his life. Not only this, but also rejoice in God through our Lord Jesus Christ through whom we have now received reconciliation.'*

All of humanity was condemned by God to eternal hell because we all belong to Adam race. Adam the first man sinned, disobeyed God, causing all of his offspring to disobey God, for all of Adam race are sinners. God the creator of the whole universe and humanity is Sovereign and his word is the perfect law. *"Justification is the sovereign work of God in which he declares the guilty sinner to be righteous and the rightful demands of the law are satisfied."*

Jesus Christ took the sins of humanity and shed his blood on the cross, and was forsaken by God and die in our place. God the Father can now credit Jesus's righteousness to us and own us as his redeemed people when we are in Jesus Christ.

God had been reconciling the whole world to himself from the moment of Adam's disobedience. You see, God had already done all the work he wanted to do before the creation of the world, so that the death and resurrection of Jesus completed the first stage of salvation of each individual who would be in Jesus. For all who had been born and had died and all who were alive at the time plus those who were yet to be born. The whole church of Jesus Christ past, present and future.

'Once you were alienated from God and were enemies in your minds because of your evil behaviour. But now he has reconciled you by Christ physical body through death to present you holy in his sight without blemish and free from accusations'.

We are told in Revelations Satan is the accuser. He accuses us before the throne of God, day and night he will accuse us by tapping into our guilty conscience and we start accusing ourselves instead of taking all to God through the power and guidance of the Holy Spirit. We must understand that God is the one who starts the process of the salvation of each individual and continues to the end our earthly life.

We have seen that the whole humanity came under Adam's curse because all are in Adam, as Adam died so all in Adam died, it is a corporate death, from the moment of birth we are dying. Christ's obedience brought the possibility of justification for all, however most of humanity will not be able to accept justification because of their sin, and therefore redemption and by Jesus Christ.

Christ's obedience in doing the will of God, going to the cross brings the gift of God to those who experience the grace of God bringing forth faith in God through Jesus Christ. With the power of the of the Holy Spirit of God empowering each individual believer. "Regeneration is the place where the work of grace begins in a sinner.". In order to respond to God we need to made alive in God only by the power of God.

Jesus gives a startling statement in John, *'Verily truly I tell you, no one can enter the Kingdom of God unless they are born of water and the Spirit.'* Jesus is talking about the regeneration of the spiritually dead person. We are all spiritually dead until the Spirit produces spiritual life and light into our human spirits then precedes down into our souls effecting our attitudes and behaviour. The Holy Spirit brings us under the hearing of the gospel of Jesus Christ.

'Faith comes from hearing the message, and the message is heard through the word about Christ.' (KJV)

It is His work to regenerate us for we are all sinners. It is the beginning of God's the work of grace in our hearts, *'I will sprinkle clean water on you and you will be clean; I will cleanse you from all your impurities and from all your idols. I will give you a new heart and put a new spirit in you, I will remove from your heart of stone and give you a heart of flesh. And I will put my Spirit in you and move you to follow my decrees and be careful to keep my laws.'*

As you can see, it begins and continues with God. God cleanse us and prepare us for the removal of the heart of stone and places in us a heart of flesh, a teachable heart. We were spiritually dead and he brings us alive by giving us new birth and we are able to respond to God through the power of the Holy Spirit. It is he who empowers us in the process, we are to turn away from sin and turn to God and we can't do this on our own, we need to be guided empowered by the Holy Spirit, we need to repent, to do a three hundred and sixty decree turn in our attitude to God and our thinking and lives.

In Acts Paul farewelling the Ephesians says something that is very important, I have declared both to Jews and Greeks, that they must turn to God in repentance and have faith in our Lord Jesus Christ. *"True repentance involves seeing sin for what it really is; not just a character defect but a permanent attitude of rebellion against the love and care and righteous authority of God. It is this new understanding of God and one's own sin that leads to repentance. Faith is an unwavering trust in the Lord Jesus Christ as the only Saviour to deal with sin."*

NOTES

Nee Watchman, The Normal Christian Life, 4th Edition,20005, America.

Jeremiah 17:9

1Peter 1:19

Peter Jeffery, Bitesize Theology, pp53 54, Bitesize Theology, EP Books England

Colossians 1:21-22

John 3:5

Romans 10:17

Ezekiel 36: 25-27

Acts 20:21

Peter Jeffery, Bitesize Theology, pp57, Bitesize Theology, EP Books England

Four

We need to ask the Father through his Spirit what he wants from each one of us. The right spiritual condition is to have Jesus Christ as our Savior and Lord of our lives.

Faith is more than an intellectual acceptance which is subjective to the individual. Faith involves the objective truth of God through the power and guidance of the Holy Spirit of God. *"Faith hears the truth of the gospel, believes it then acts upon it. Saving faith progresses from a belief in certain facts to a real trusting in Christ and what he has done on our behalf and for our salvation."* It can only come about by the power and guidance of the Holy Spirit who guides us in allowing ourselves to respond. *"Faith is a response of the mind and heart to the Saviour of whom the gospel speaks."*

The foreknowledge of the Father knew that the Son was willing to come and be the sacrifice for sinful humanity. 'Who have been chosen,(God's children), according to foreknowledge of God the Father through the sanctifying work of the Spirit, to be obedient to Jesus Christ.' And he knew those who would be drawn by the Holy Spirit into the new covenant in the blood of Jesus Christ.

The Holy Spirit continues his work in us continually bringing us to repentance everyday as continuing sinners saved only by the grace of God. As we are obedient and willing, we need to be continually asking Him to guide us each day in our battle with sin. And when we fail which, we will continually to do, He will guide us in our confession to the Father in the name of Jesus Christ.

We must accept that we will never stop sinning this side of glory for we are born of Adam. This is something that many Christians especially new Christians can have big problem with. They find it very difficult to accept that they will continually sin ask for forgiveness and sin again, *'Therefore, just as sin entered the world through one man and death through sin and in the same way death came to all men(peoples) because all have sinned.'*

When we belong to God, we are infused with empowering hope that will not disappoint us by empowerment of the Holy Spirit, *'Now if we have died with Christ, we believe that we will also live with him. For we know Christ was raised from the dead, he cannot die again; death no longer has mastery over him. The death he died, he died to sin once for all; but the life he lives, he lives to God. In the same way count yourselves dead to sin but alive to God in Christ Jesus.'*

As Christ fully identified himself with us humans even to taking on the power of sin, which did not master him. He was completely able to die to sin and to rise to bring the resurrection life to those who believe on his name, *'God made him (Jesus), who had no sin to be sin to be sin for us, so that in him we might become the righteousness of God'.*

The sin we are to die to in the name of Jesus Christ is the power of sin, the life we are to live in Jesus Christ through the indwelling power of the Holy Spirit gives us the empowerment of the willing obedience of Jesus to God the Father, *'Likewise, reckon yourselves to be dead to sin but alive unto God through Jesus Christ our Lord.'* The word reckon is to do with accounting it is a verb, to do, adding up the numbers and reconciling the account books. In doing the books of our life in Jesus Christ through guidance of the Holy Spirit, we must allow him to empower us to consider ourselves dead to sin and be empowered alive to God, Father, Son and of course the Holy Spirit.

The power of the indwelling of the Holy Spirit is the power of transformation, *'Do not be conformed to the pattern of this world, but be transformed by the renewing of your mind'* The qualifying spiritual renewal that the Holy Spirit implants in the human spirits of those who have become believers to starts the progress down from our human spirit and into the mind of the individuals causing changes in pattern of thinking and living, empowering the heart and character of each Christian.

The life we are to live now in the Spirit takes us on the journey of dying with Christ to sin, *'Since you have taken off your old self with its practices and put on the new self which is being renewed in the image of its creator.'* This resurrection life changes our relationship to God, to ourselves and to sin. We need to be living this new life in Jesus Christ in the now.

Living life in Jesus Christ as the children of God, we do this in the spiritual positiveness of manner only in Jesus Christ and through the guidance of the Holy Spirit of God in our hearts and attitude of thinking. The Holy Spirit takes us on the journey of the willingness of Christ's righteousness, where we are willing slaves to righteousness and obedience to God the Father. *'Don't you know that when you offer yourselves to someone as obedient slaves, you are slaves of the one you obey; whether you are a slave to sin, which leads to death, or to obedience which leads to righteousness? But thanks be to God that though you used to be a slave to sin, you have come to obey from your heart the pattern of teaching that has now claimed your allegiance. You have been set free from sin and have become slaves to righteousness.'*

The word 'slave', used to be abhorrent to people of the democratic western world however, more and more socially economic persons both male and female are using those who are not so well off as slaves these days. However, the fact is we are either a slave to sin and therefore a slave to Satan and death or are guided through the Holy Spirit to be obedient to Jesus Christ and therefore a slave to righteousness and life. The Son of God went into the slave market of the world and bought back for God the Father children with his precious blood from the slave trader Satan, *'Therefore, I urge you brothers and sisters, in view of God's mercy, offer your bodies as living sacrifices, holy and pleasing to God, this is your true and proper worship.'*

The Apostle Paul was urging the readers of his letters and us today to respond to transforming power of the Gospel of

Jesus Christ, through the indwelling of the Holy Spirit. As Christians we are to be slaves of Christ.

In Romans times if a slave loved his master and wanted to stay as his master's slave for the rest of his life, he would get his master to punch a hole in his earlobe. When we truly are Christians we are to be slaves of Christ, today and rest of our lives but, it has to be only God the Father's way, not ours. For God the Father, the Person who planned our creation and our salvation, and the Son who procured it by shedding his blood for us, loves us his children with an eternal love.

In order, to love Jesus Christ and be his slave, we need the Person of the Holy Spirit. The Triune God is God the Father, God the Son and God the Holy Spirit. *'If you love me, keep my commands. And I will ask the Father and He will give you another Advocate, (Counselor and Paraclete) to help you and be with you forever, the Spirit of Truth. The world cannot accept Him, it neither see Him or knows Him. But you know Him for He lives with you and will in you. I will not leave you as orphans, I will come to you. But the Advocate, Holy Spirit, whom the Father will send in my name, will teach you all things and remind you of everything I have said to you.'*

The Holy Spirit is sent to believers by the Father and the Son, He takes up residence in the heart each believer.

For when the Holy Spirit is dwelling in the believer the Triune God, is there. There can only one God dwelling there for it is a single dwelling place. No other gods can occupy the heart as well.

NOTES

Peter Jeffery, Bitesize Theology, pp58, Bitesize Theology, EP Books England

Peter Jeffery, Bitesize Theology, pp58, Bitesize Theology, EP Books England

1Peter 1:2

Romans 5:12

Romans 6:8-11

2Corinthians 5:21

King James Bible; Romans 6:11

Romans 12:2

Colossians 3:9-10

Romans 12:1

Romans 6:16-18

John 14:15-18, 26

Five

There is one thing that we, modern day Christians can find hard to accept is that God allows believers trials to sift our faith. God is the Master Craftsman. He examines his creations for defect causes, because of sin. He works through a of process of repair and strengthening us in spiritual resilience to do the work he has in mind for each one of us. *'But when you are tempted, he will also provide a way you can endure.'*

Objective faith through Jesus Christ enables each one of us, a child of God, to endure through the empowering of the Holy Spirit, in whatever situation we find ourselves. This the conviction of truth, is based on the reality of the resurrection of Jesus Christ. The actuality is factual-based truth of the resurrection of Jesus Christ.

It brings about a willing obedience through the guidance of the Holy Spirit to the reality of the Truth, who is Jesus Christ. *'Faith is being sure of what we hope for and certain of what we do not see'.* The evidence of our faith can only be seen in our attitudes, behavior and deeds based on what God has guided each one of his children to know through the empowerment of his Holy Spirit to our hearts. Our attitude is to bring glory and honour to his holy name. It is not what we think our life is supposed to be, it is what God knows our life is needs to be. This can only happen if the Holy Spirit is dwelling in each one of us producing a crop of deeds. Otherwise, our faith is inactive consequentially it is dead, *'As the body without the spirit is dead, so faith without deeds is dead.'*

The behavior of the child of God requires the wisdom from above to have a godly attitude, willing and obedient heart and a life that brings glory to God the Father. It is too easy to be conned especially by those who give the impression that they love God and are willing and obedient to God, but consider God and his children as complete idiots.

The Holy Spirit producing the Fruit of the Spirit in us. *'The fruit of the Spirit is love, joy, peace, patience, kindness, goodness, faithfulness, gentleness and self-control'.*

Bringing about the inspiration, motivation and stimulus of obedience and worship that can only come from God guiding us to ask for his wisdom through the Holy Spirit, empowering us to allow him produce a crop of righteousness.

In order, to allow the Holy Spirit to produce this crop we must be willing and obedient to God by faith in Christ. Called to understanding, that we are not captains of our souls *'Trust in the Lord with all your heart and lean not on your own understanding; in all your ways submit to him and he will make your paths straight. Do not be wise in your own eyes, fear the Lord and shun evil.'*

To shun evil we must be willing and obedient to God through the power of the Holy Spirit in the name of Jesus Christ. This is what brings freedom to live the Christian life. We must not allow ourselves to be deceived by Satan and his servants in our thinking for, until we go to be with the Lord, we will continue to have an attitude towards sin. Instead of considering ourselves boss of our lives, even when we say we are Christians, we are still opening the door up for Satan into our beings and lives. We need to allow God and his will for us to have first place, *'Submit yourselves then to God. Resist the devil and he will flee from you. Come near to God and he will come near to you.'*

Jesus and his disciples including Paul, are examples for us modern Christians to follow through the guidance of the Holy Spirit. When Jesus was cleansing the temple of the money changes in, the disciples remembered a verse, zeal for your house consumes me. The English word zeal, translated in the Greek, to *zelos,* meaning, passion, dedication and enthusiasm in the positive. The temple was the place where the ordinary people could meet with their God and it is understandable that Jesus would have a great zeal for the temple that consumed him. Today, we his people, who are indwelt by the Holy Spirit come together as his body to worship him as one.

On the day of Pentecost not only were all the disciples empowered by the Holy Spirit to speak languages that they had not learnt in order to spread the gospel of Jesus Christ, Peter was zealously embolden to get up and speak to the Jews who were listening about what God through Jesus and the Holy Spirit had just done, He had started to feed the flock. Then years later Peter writing to the scattered Christians to encourage them in their behaviour of their most holy faith to their God and brothers and sisters. *'Be shepherds of God flock which is under your care serving as overseers, not because you must but because you are willing.'*

The conversion of Paul from a non-beliver to a believer in Jesus Christ was very dramatic bringing a spiritual zeal that all consume him with a dedication and passion that would carry him all through all that God the Father would allow to happen to him in oder to carry out his will. For Father God is jealous for his children for he knows the best way for them, which is in Jesus Christ, for we certainly do not know without the guidance of the Holy Spirit. We can see an illustration of God's jealousy for his people in Paul, who was the apostle to the Gentiles, in which the church of today is part of. Paul writing to the Christian, *'I am jealous for you with a godly jealously. I promised you to one husband, Christ, so that I might present you as a virgin to him. But I am afraid that just Eve was deceived by the serpent's cunning your minds somehow be led astray from your sincere and pure devotion to Christ.'*

In this day an age of the planting of weeds among the seeds, we are easily led and deceived as Eve was. We have no idea of what real truth is, it is chocked out of us. Today's Christians are children of this present age, like Eve we are easily deceived. However, that is not to say that previous generations were any better.

Objective truth comes only from God though the indwelling of the Holy Spirit bringing faith and hope in God, *'Now we are children of God, what we will be has not* been made known. But we know when he appears we shall be like him for we shall see him as he is. Everyone who has this hope in him(Jesus) purifies himself, just as he is pure.'

As believers we have the Holy Spirit living in us, who is the Spirit of Christ bringing hope of renewal of spirit soul and body when Jesus Christ returns, 'The Lord Jesus Christ, who by the power that enables him to bring everything under his control will transform our lowly bodies so that we will be like him.'

This empowerment of the Holy Spirit starts the longing for a deeper worship of God, not the continual external fleetingness of the old man, 'You were taught with regard to your former way of life, to put off your old self, which is being corrupted by it's deceitful desires, to be made new in the attitude of your minds; and to put on the new self, created to be like God in true righteousness and holiness.' When we become a child of God, the old self starts to become obsolete.

As children of God we need to concentrate on allowing the Spirit to work on our character in the process of metamorphosis, to change our complete pattern of soulical thought and the thinking of our minds. To allow the Spirit to lead us in divine insight and disclosure, not what we think, but God knows. 'Since you have taken off the old self and have put on the new self which is being *renewed in knowledge, in the image of it's creator'.* You are therefore qualified and made new in the image of the Son.

As a sinner saved only by the grace of God, I defiantly still need the process of metamorphosis of my soulical pattern of thought and the thinking of my mind to continue until the Father takes me home. The power of sin is like a car idling, just waiting to get on the road again, however continuation of the process of the breaking down the old man renders the power of sin less and less, even though it doesn't go away this side of our resurrection

We who are believers have been adopted by God to be his adopted children through the Son, Jesus Christ, *'For those who are led by the Spirit of God are the children of God. The Spirit you received does not make you a slave, so that you live in fear again, rather the Spirit you received brought about your adoption to sonship. And by him we cry Abba Father. The Spirit himself testifies with our spirit that we are God's children. Now if we are children, then we are heirs, heirs of God and co-heirs with Christ.'* The Spirit brings about a realisation of awareness, through the Spirit of adoption that we have a commitment to God and only to God.

We see this happened without our involvement before the beginning of the world, which brings great hope, *'For he chose us in him (Jesus), before the creation of the world, to be holy and blameless in his sight. In love he predestined us to be adopted as his sons(and daughters) through Jesus Christ in accordance with his pleasure and will.'* God adopted us believers in Jesus into sonship before the creation of the world to partake as heirs in eternal salvation.

Adoption in Romans times when there was no male heir, it was quite involved, there was at least two or three different ways. We will look at the last one, which had two stages to it. *"Under Roman law the first stage involved the destruction of paternal power of the previous father. The second stage involved the new relationship with new father and the establishment of his fatherly powers."*

In this day and age we don't have to be a male to receive the full rights of sonship in Jesus Christ, we are to be daughters as well. *'To redeem those under the law, that we might receive the full rights of sons. Because you are sons, God sent the Spirit of his Son into our hearts, the Spirit who call out, Abba Father. So you are no longer a slave, but a son; and since you are a son, God has also made you an heir.'*

Before the beginning of the world, before the creation of one human being, God predestined by divine election believers, based only on his grace, nothing to do with us humans at all. What for?' For he chose us in him (Son) before the creation of the world to be holy and blameless in his sight.'

In Peter's letter, he starts by mentioning what God has already done, the death and resurrection of Jesus Christ. Bringing about the introduction of new birth of the children of God in the new covenant in the blood of Jesus Christ, *'Praise be to God and Father of our Lord Jesus Christ. In his great mercy he has given us new birth into a living hope through the resurrection of Jesus Christ from the dead, and into an inheritance that can never perish, spoil or fade in heaven for you, who through faith are shielded by God's power until the coming of salvation that is already to be revealed in the last time.'* This new birth in Jesus has change each person into a child of God with a citizenship in the Kingdom of God and a new relationship with the Triune God and an eternal inheritance.

God the Father has lavished on us this blessedness in Christ Jesus according to his great pleasure in all Godly wisdom through the power of the Holy Spirit. For a life pleasing to God, *'And we pray this in order that you may live a life worthy of the Lord and may please him in every way, bearing fruit in every good work, growing in the knowledge of God, being strengthened with all power according to his glorious might so that you may have great endurance and patience and joyfully give thanks to the Father who has qualified you to share in the inheritance of the saints in the Kingdom of Light.'*

We are to be completely-filled up and used of the Holy Spirit, spirit, soul and physical body. The Father gives all his children a way to proceed in our daily lives through the power of the Holy Spirit. We need to be in a close relationship with Father, we are not perfect, we will never be perfect this side of going home. The Father has always known this. He will continue work, guide and empower us through his Holy Spirit to bring about his will in each one of us to live worthy of the Lord and to know God more deeply for to know God is life eternal.

However, you may be saying as I do sometimes, I have a terrible life but Jesus told the disciple and us, *'In this world you will have trouble. But take heart, I have overcome the world.'* So we are to move and have our beings in Christ Jesus, meaning spiritual and eternal but also recovering and transitioning spiritually, soulical and physical, further into our relationship with the Father. We are being changed from the old man into the new, we don't know what we will be, but God certainly knows.

NOTES

1Corinthians 10:13

Hebrews 11:.1

James 2:26

Galatians 5:22-23,

Proverbs 3:5-7,

James 4:7

John 2:17

1Peter 5:2-3

2Corinthians 11:2-3,

1John, 3:2-3

Philippians 3:21

Ephesians 4:22-23

Colossians 3:9

Romans 8:14-17

Ephesians 1:4-5

Phil Davis, The Father I Never Knew, pp 48, 1991, NavPress, Colorado Springs

Galatians 4:5-7

Ephesians 1:4

1Peter 1:3-5

Colossians 1:10-12

John 16:33

Act17:28

Six

There is a hymn that encourages us to, worship the Lord in the beauty of holiness. Bow down before him the Lord is his name. However, we can't do this on our own the bible tells us how it happens, *'May God himself, the God of peace sanctify you through and through. May your whole spirit, soul and body be kept blameless at the coming of our Lord Jesus Christ.'*

It is God alone who sanctifies us, calls us, makes us holy, spiritually separated to be in a relationship with the Triune God, Father, Son and Holy Spirit. It is to be a holistic approach, to our spirit, soul and body to worship God in our everyday lives. This is done through the power and guidance of the Holy Spirit in us, living God-pleasing lives as our daily worship, with sacrifices and service to God as we interact with the world around us.

One of our biggest problems is ourselves, we tend to go off in tandems thinking what we think is what God knows and is thinking, telling God we know what is right. In our so-called modern independent world where there are many who call themselves Christians, but have no resemblances to what may be called an everyday sinful Christian, saved only by the grace of God.

When in fact the worship and service we are to offer to God is to bring glory to him, not to ourselves, *'Therefore. I urge you brothers (sisters) in view of God's mercy to offer your bodies as living sacrifices, holy and pleasing to God, this is your spiritual act of worship.'* As we view God's mercies to us, the Holy Spirit encourages and empowers us to move through the Spirit to offer ourselves to God in whatever way he knows it is the best way for us to go.

Johnson says, "The God who is love, draws near to me, a sinful, mere mortal, to draw me near to himself, in order to draw me within the circle of Love itself."

Our grateful response to God each and everyday, is to worship him and to be responsive in service to our God in whatever way he guides and moves us. Paul writing to the Corinthians expresses these words, *'This service you perform is not only supplying the needs of God's people but is also overflowing in many expressions of thanks to God. Because of the service by which you have proved yourselves, men will praise God for the obedience that accompanies your confession of the gospel of Christ.'* At times we have many expressions of thanks!

Torance says, "Are they an appropriate response to the gospel? Do they help people to apprehend the worship and ministry of Christ as he draws us by the Spirit into a life of shared communion, or do they hinder?"

The benefits for those who not only believe in Jesus Christ but also whom, the Father deems to be his own are encouraged, *'Let us draw near to God with sincere hearts in full assurance of faith having our hearts sprinkled to cleanse us from a guilty conscience and having our bodies washed with pure water. Let us hold unswervingly to the hope we profess, for he who promised is faithful.'* This hope we profess is because God himself has promised and he is faithful, not us.

The first benefits is of the indwelling the Holy Spirit causing us be spiritually alive and empowering us to be able to worship God in the beauty of holiness. For we are being continually sanctified, being brought further and further into this relationship with the Triune God who is bringing us closer and closer to the goal of the completion of our salvation of being holy and blameless in the sight of God.

Even though I was a child of God my heart wasn't where God wanted my heart to be, my heart was on the path of the hard place. And it was a down trodden place, for a downtrodden heart to be. I took the worldly way even though I thought God was in this, of studying and working and doing and doing but he was not. Friends were encouraging me that I needed to tell the Holy Spirit to give me this and that. I was saying to God do I need what-so-ever, please guide in the way you want me to go. After some time he showed me that they were saying, what was prosperity doctrine and that this was not of God.

Nevertheless, God was working in me through his Spirit guiding me in the way he wanted me to go in spite of myself and the illnesses, coming one after another. He gave me, *'continue to work out your salvation with fear and trembling, for it is God who works in you to will and to, act according to his good pleasure.'* The Spirit showed me that my so-called obedience wasn't of God's good pleasure at all. He is the only one who produces salvation and the continual salvation in the individual.

I needed to confess to the Father my sin and ask him through the guidance of the Spirit in my attitude and soulical thinking. In the name of Jesus Christ. And with the indwelling empowerment of the Holy Spirit I started to experience the deliverance of God. However, it wasn't the way I would have thought it would be. I had already spent a couple times in hospital and I needed to continue in his way.

I believe that God through his Spirit gave me, *'And we know that in all things God works for good of those who love him, who have been called according to his purpose. For those God foreknew he also predestined to be conformed to the likeness of his Son, that he might be the firstborn among many brothers'.*

I was saying to the Father, I don't know that all things work for good, for they don't seem to be at that time, for I didn't have access to what I needed to know and so I asked the Father how I could access such understanding? Through the Spirit eventually I was able to the access I needed. The word for 'know' in Greek is, *odia*, meaning, intimate knowledge, to respect, to adore, a willing obedience as Jesus had. The Spirit was showing me that needed to start asking the Father for a willing obedience and also healing and then the slow progression off the medication that was really coated poison. The Father went ahead of me and when I had to go to hospital five years later for something else where I had to have many tests, I was told I was healed from the other and they recommended that the doctor I had at time would send me to a specialist, who was able to say that I was well and took me off the medication, in that slow progression that was needed.

The Spirit progressionally works in the believer, it is not like, *ginosko*, which means to acquire knowledge which is subjective to the individual. I must admit that I was gob-smacked, to think that God was working for my beneficial good in allowing all that was happening. He foreknew in eternity past, and predestines each individual believer to know through the indwelling of the Holy Spirit in an intimate relationship with the living God and eternal salvation in and through Jesus Christ. The spiritual deliverance that brings eternal life.

God issues an invitation to all humans through the Spirit, however we are to be responsible for our decisions. God made all humans with a free will to accept, however as we have seen not many will accept the invitation, *'Many are invited but few are chosen'.* But those who do accept God's invitation, which has to be on God's terms. The Spirit empowers believers to be willingly to accept the idea of complete salvation, and the Godly consequences in God in the name of Jesus Christ.

God the Father didn't go, 'I'll take that one but leave that one'. No. God knew in eternity past those who would accept the invitation on his terms. In other word, chosen by God and taken out of the kingdom of the world and taken into the Kingdom of God in the name of Jesus Christ by the empowerment of God's Holy Spirit before the creation of the world, which was to be God's ultimate goal.

NOTES

1 Thessalonians 5:23

Romans 12:1

Johnson Darrell, Experiencing The Trinity, 1947, pp63, Regent
Publishing

2 Corinthians 9: 12-13

Torrance J B, p 15,1996, Inter Varsity Press, Illinois.

Hebrews 10:22-23

Ephesians 1L4

Philippians 2:12-13

Romans 8:28-29

Matthew 22:14

seven

I n the conformity to the Son we must realise we are spiritually helpless, we cannot help ourselves. Frank Cooke says, "Those who are perceptive enough to know their need. To know him and our total dependence on him, is bliss indeed."

Fortunate, are the poor in spirit, for theirs is the Kindgom of Heaven. The poor in spirit realise they need God desperately, for they are spiritually helpless. God through the Holy Spirit comes to dwell in each one of us bringing the dawn of the Kingdom and bring the beginning of spiritual resilience.

Destined are those who mourn for they will comforted by God. We have to admit our sin, to God and also, especially to ourselves. Confessing our critical need of God as our constant companion. Comforted by the Holy Spirit means being fortified — strengthened as if within a fortress. It is a divine reinforcement. *'Blessed are the meek, for they will inherit the earth.'* Meekness is a life of discipline and self-control, empowered by God's Spirit and sustained by His grace. It shapes our attitude toward God and others, reflecting trust in His perfect goodness and love. The meek are not weak, but those who know how to harness strength under God's control.

Heaven-sent, those who hunger and thirst for righteousness. *'Give us our daily bread'.* Righteousness belongs to God, in order to belong to God we need to conform to his belonging, his moral honesty is not ours, however he does proportion his honesty through the empowerment of his Holy Spirit to those are in this relationship.

The kindhearted are blessed, they will be shown mercy. The believer who has been shown mercy by God through the Holy Spirit needs to show thankful mercy to their fellow human being. The pure in heart will see God, the spiritually unadulterated. In today world the word pure has been degraded, however it means washed and clean in pure water.

Paul finishing his letter to the Ephesians by encouraging them and everyone of us to put on the armour of God.

'Finally, be strong in the Lord and his mighty power. Put on the full armour of God, so that you can take your stand against the devil's schemes.' To accept the empowerment of the Holy Spirit in our spirits and souls fortifying us with Jesus' willing obedience to the Father.

Paul tells us that we are to be strong in God's awesome magnificence power that is beyond compare. The power we have been equipped for our struggle against sin and Satan is the very same power that brought Christ back from the dead.

This fortifying empowerment of the Holy Spirit gives us the willing obedience of Christ to empower us to allow ourselves to be raise from the dead when we are called by God. *'And if the Spirit of him who raised Jesus from the dead is living in you, he who raised Christ from the dead will also give life to your mortal bodies through his Spirit who lives in you.'*

God the Father called us to be created, he called us to be born again and he will call us home to be with him forever.

In reality God's power is not something we can tap into, as we were in charge of the process, rather, it is something, inevitably at work within all those whom God has chosen and called. When reading our Bibles, we consider that we are the ones who is doing it, therefore we are usually so proud of what we have achieved or because we have not failed God, who may have given up on us, Most time we forget to include the Holy Spirit anyway.

God has done his part perfectly in making the armour available, now it is up to us to choose whether to use it, we are often unwilling and unable even to think clearly about the armour let alone put it on.

It is the Holy Spirit who empowers us to remember to ask the Father in the name of Jesus Christ to arm us with the armor of God.

The armour that the Holy Spirit clothes us in is the armour that the Son wore, *'Righteousness will be his belt and faithfulness will be his sash around his waist.'*

The Spirit clothe us so that the righteousness and faithfulness will also becomes the belt of truth, part of the armour of God. 'Stand firm then with the belt of truth buckled around your waist', Jesus' orderly way of truth is objective. For he is Truth. He continually stopped Satan in his tracks. When Satan came to him tempted him, to turn stones into bread, Jesus said, *'Man shall not live by bread alone but by every word that comes from the mouth of God.'*

As you Jesus surround my whole being with yourself. You who are truth. Please buckle the Belt of Truth around my waist, that I will think and admit only your Truth in my inner place. You dear Jesus are the Righteousness of God. Please be my Righteousness, for I have none except what You give me and protect my heart from all unrighteousness. *'With the breastplate of righteousness in place',* This is Jesus' breastplate, *'He will put on righteousness as his breastplate and the helmet of salvation on his head.'* No- one can deliver us from the most powerful enemy, Satan and sin, only Jesus can. 'God made him who knew no sin to be sin for us, so that in him we might become the righteousness of God'

For people like us, the breastplate of righteousness is really good news. It declares that no matter how bad you have been, the offer of God's deliverance still stands.

I pray in the name of Jesus Christ that you Almighty God will put on my feet the preparation of the Gospel of peace. *'Our feet fitted with the readiness that comes from the gospel of peace'.* We need to accept God's terms of peace. We ourselves are the first people who need to hear this good news of peace. We often don't have the unshakable peace that the gospel should bring us.

However, most of the time we don't have peace with God and ourselves and so we find it near impossible to talk to others about Jesus.

In the name of Jesus, I pray that you dear Father will put on my arm the shield of faith, in Christ Jesus to protect me from Satan's fiery darts, all principalities, compromising, deception gossip, spiritual wickedness, slander, rulers of darkness, doubt and unbelief. Faith is the means by which we flee to God for refuge. It is how we cling to God and find in him the comfort and protection in the times of difficultly and distress.

Faith has to built on the Truth, Jesus. Jesus said to the disciples in *'I am the way and the truth, and the life, no-one comes to the Father except by me.'*

By faith, we lay hold of truth reminding ourselves of the promises of God. God has promised to be with me when I walk through the deep and desperate trials.

Since we belong to the day, let us be self-controlled, putting on faith and love as a breastplate and the hope of salvation as a helmet. For God did not appoint us to suffer wrath but to receive salvation through our Lord Jesus Christ. We are to take the helmet salvation in the name of Jesus. We experience God's power, spiritually and eternally that he bestows on his children. *'Since we belong to the day let us be self-control putting on faith and love as a breastplate and the hope of salvation as a helmet.'*

The believer's relationship with Jesus Christ is set apart through the empowerment of the Holy Spirit, from the worldly ideas of what Christianity is supposed to be like.

Hope is a settled conviction about where we will spend eternity. Biblical hope is sufficiently sure that you can give a reason for. *'Set apart Christ as Lord. Always be prepared to give an answer to everyone who asks you to give the reason for the hope that you have. But do this with gentleness and respect.'*

The Word of God in it's cleansing work serves as a set of shears, a scalpel, and a sword. *'I am the true Vine and my Father is the Gardener. He cuts off every branch that bears no fruit while every branch that bears fruit He prunes so that it will be even more fruitful.'* The gardener using shears prunes the vine in order for more fruit

God the Father Is the complete and ultimate authority of the universe. It is He who judges if a person belongs to him in Jesus Christ. It is defiantly not us humans who might say that we are a Christians. It is Jesus who brings the person to the God the Father and it is He who conveys to the Son if this person has been adopted by the Father into Jesus Christ.

There is the third Person of the Trinity, the Holy Spirit who uses the scalpel. God through the Holy Spirit uses the scalpel to operate and convict us of sin.

The surgeon's knife just not cutting for the sake of making a wound. It cuts to save the whole body by taking out the diseased part. Also the scalpel of the Holy Spirit doesn't just cut us so that God can watch us bleed. The Holy Spirit comes to convict the world(and us) not just about sin but also righteousness.

'When he comes, he, the Holy Spirit, will convict the world of guilt in regard to sin and righteousness and judgement.' The Holy Spirit convicts us of our constant rebelling against God the Father to empower us with the willingness of Jesus Christ in our hearts and minds.

We need to take out the Sword of the Spirit, God's word and study it, memorise it and immerse ourselves in it. In other words do sword drills for the sword of the Spirit is the only defensive weapon we have, it belongs to the Holy Spirit for the children of to use. *'All scripture is God-breathed and is useful for teaching, rebuking, correcting and training in righteousness, so that the man (women) of God may be throughly equipped for every good work'.*

Every believer needs to know how use the word in the correct way and manner, *'For though we live in the world, we do not wage war as the world does, The weapons we fight with are not the weapons of this world, On the contrary they have divine power to demolish strongholds. We demolish arguments and every pretensions that sets it's itself up against the knowledge of God and we take captive every though and make it obedient to Christ'.*

Jesus Christ is life to all humanity, especially to all believers. He is the Source of life to all who believe on his name. The Holy Spirit who is the Spirit of Christ, is the Sword of God. He will accomplish what God the Father has willed. *'The word of God is living and active. Sharper than any double-edged sword, it penetrates, even to soul and spirit, joints and marrow, it judges the thoughts and attitudes of the heart. Nothing in all creation is hidden God's sight. Everything is uncovered and laid bare before the eyes of him to whom we must give account.'*

The soul in the self- awareness, tends to focus on self. The human spirit is where God meets with all believers, it is the God awareness of the human being. The joints and marrow, the physical being. The Holy Spirit brings unity to human spirit and soul causing our hearts to be open to God and our attitudes and motives be examine by God in order that we move and have our beings in Jesus Christ. Even though we spoke of the sword of the Spirit in the previous chapter as our defence weapon. There is a more effective weapon and that is pray, especially under the control guidance of the Spirit of God who takes pray to a higher level of efficiency. Prayer is not so much another weapon that the Christian has been given as it is the means by which all of his or her weaponry is kept effective under the control and guidance of God.

It has been stated before, that we are not captains of our souls or master of our fate, we must be totally dependent on God otherwise there can't be a relationship with the Triune God. *'And we know that in all things God works for good of those who love him, who have been called according to his purpose.'* The most important characteristic for our prayers is that they are to be in the Spirit having a strong relationship with God and praying in the Holy Spirit is not a mystical experience but rather prayer that is prompted and guided by the Holy Spirit.

This needs to be our war cry. Jesus Christ is my hero.

NOTES

Cooke F, Jesus Ru;es OK, pp22-23, Henry Walter, 1978

Cooke F, Jesus Ru;es OK, pp25, Henry Walter, 1978

Cooke F, Jesus Ru;es OK, pp27, Henry Walter, 1978

Matthew 6:11

Ephesians 6:10-11

Duguid Iain, pp13-14, 2019, Crossway Publishing,

Romans 8:11,

Duguid Iain, p15, 2019, Crossway Publishing

Duguid Iain, p14-15, 2019, Crossway Publishing

Isaiah 11:5

Ephesians 6-14

Ephesians 6:14

Matthew 4-4

Isaiah 59:17

2Corinthians5:21

Duguid Iain, p43, 2019, Crossway Publishing

Ephesians 6:15

Duguid Iain, p59, 2019, Crossway Publishing

Duguid Iain, p68, 2019, Crossway Publishing

John 14:6,

Duguid Iain, p72, 2019, Crossway Publishing

1Thessalonians 5: 8-9,

Duguid Iain, p79, 2019, Crossway Publishing 1Peter 3:15

Duguid Iain, p98 2019, Crossway Publishing

John 15:1-2

Duguid Iain, p101, 2019, Crossway Publishing

John 16:8

2 Timothy 3:16-17

2Corinthians 10:3-5

Hebrews 4: 12-13

Duguid Iain, p104, 2019, Crossway Publishing

Romans 8;28